P9-EKE-638

CH

I CAN MAKE A DIFFERENCE!

Jessica Pegis

Crabtree Publishing Company
www.crabtreebooks.com

Author: Jessica Pegis

Series research and development: Reagan Miller

Editors: Petrice Custance and Reagan Miller

Proofreader: Janine Deschenes

Design and photo research: Margaret Amy Salter

Prepress technician: Margaret Amy Salter

Print and production coordinator: Katherine Berti

Photographs

Shutterstock.com: Ms Jane Campbell: page 13 (left);
    Orlok: page 16 (bottom right)
Wikimedia Commons: Moving Mountains Trust: page 19

All other images from Shutterstock

Library and Archives Canada Cataloguing in Publication

Pegis, Jessica, author
    I can make a difference! / Jessica Pegis.

(Citizenship in action)
Includes index.
Issued in print and electronic formats.
ISBN 978-0-7787-2599-2 (hardback).--
ISBN 978-0-7787-2605-0 (paperback).--
ISBN 978-1-4271-1776-2 (html)

    1. Political participation--Juvenile literature. 2. Social
participation--Juvenile literature. I. Title.

JF799.P44 2016   j323'.042   C2016-904144-1
                                           C2016-904145-X

Library of Congress Cataloging-in-Publication Data

CIP available at the Library of Congress

Crabtree Publishing Company

www.crabtreebooks.com   1-800-387-7650

Printed in Canada/082016/TL20160715

Published in Canada
Crabtree Publishing
616 Welland Ave.
St. Catharines, Ontario
L2M 5V6

Published in the United States
Crabtree Publishing
PMB 59051
350 Fifth Avenue, 59th Floor
New York, New York 10118

Published in the United Kingdom
Crabtree Publishing
Maritime House
Basin Road North, Hove
BN41 1WR

Published in Australia
Crabtree Publishing
3 Charles Street
Coburg North
VIC 3058

What is in this book?

Citizens make a difference

Being a **citizen** means being part of a **community**. A community is a place where people live, work, and play.

Some communities are small, like a family. Other communities are big, such as a country. The whole world is another kind of community, with Earth as its home.

Citizens make their communities special by making a difference. How do citizens make a difference? By helping each other!

Citizens work hard to make their communities great places to live for everyone. Citizens do this in many ways, such as helping their neighbors shovel snow or picking up garbage in parks.

What does making a difference mean?

Citizens make a difference in their communities by:

- ✓ Talking to other people and listening to their problems

- ✓ Asking questions to better understand their problems

- ✓ Taking action to try to help solve their problems

Juan returns to school after having his tonsils removed. He tells Katie it made him sad that there weren't many toys in the hospital for him and the other children to play with.

"Why did it make you sad?" asks Katie.

"I was sad because having more toys to play with would have helped me miss my family less," says Juan.

"I have an idea," says Katie. "Let's collect toys and donate them to the hospital. We can help other kids not be sad."

"Great idea," says Juan. "We can make a difference!"

How can you make a difference?

There are many ways that you can make a difference.

In a small community, such as your family, you can show your loved ones you care for them by helping with the recycling or doing the dishes.

In a larger community, such as your school, you can make a difference by standing up to a bully.

What do you think?

Imagine you had a chance to change your community! You could change something big or small. Your change must improve people's lives. Your decision would be final for one day. After one day, your community would vote on whether to keep your idea. What would you do to make a difference?

Making a difference at home

You can make a big difference at home by doing something without being asked.

Maybe you have toys you no longer use. You could collect them in a box to give away. You could tidy up a messy bookshelf. At dinnertime, you could set the table.

Learning to **compromise** is another way to make a difference. Sometimes two people want to use the computer or watch television at the same time. This can lead to an argument.

By talking to the other person, you can agree on how to share the computer or television.

Making a difference at school

One way to make a difference at school is by showing everyone **respect**. When you show respect to your teacher and fellow students, you help make school a great place for everyone. Good citizens treat everyone as important members of the community. They listen when others are speaking.

Good citizens also take action. If they see a problem, they try to fix it. If they feel something is unfair, they speak up. You can be a good citizen and make a difference in your school today!

You can speak up and hold a **protest**.

You can tell a bully to stop.

Neighborhood Watch!

There are people in your community who need help. Some kids need clothing. Others need school supplies to start school. Some seniors need help with yard work or shoveling snow.

There are many groups that help people in your community. You can donate money or **volunteer** to help with these groups.

What do you think?

Olivia and Mark want to help people in their community. They decide to find a group they can volunteer with. Olivia and Mark plan to find the groups that are in their community by:

1 Using the Internet

2 Looking up information at the library

3 Asking their teacher or school principal

How else can Olivia and Mark find groups to volunteer with in their community?

Going Global

You can make a difference for people around the world!

You can hold a **fundraiser** and use the money to help a community in Africa get clean water.

You can help **refugees** who come to your country by being their friend. Refugees are citizens who must leave their own country because of war or severe weather.

How do you decide how to help others?

You can suggest to your teacher that your whole class should make a difference. Each student in your class can discuss a way to help others. Everyone should get a chance to speak and share an idea. Your teacher can write all the ideas on the board. Then everyone in the class will **vote** for the idea they like best.

How would you like to make a difference?

Kids Make a Difference

Sometimes you can make a difference doing something you love. Abigail Lupi loves to sing and dance. She began performing at a local senior home. Her shows made the senior citizens so happy that Abigail decided to start a group called CareGirlz. CareGirlz sing and dance at different senior homes and children's hospitals. Now Abigail is making many people happy!

Do you love working on computers? How can you use this skill or one of your other talents to help others?

This is what making a difference looks like! Students in Solio learn math in a newly built classroom.

Sometimes you can make a difference on the other side of the world. Students from Ottawa, Canada learned there were students in Solio, Kenya who only had dusty tents for classrooms. This made it hard for the students in Solio to do their schoolwork. The Canadian students decided they wanted to help. They held a fundraiser and earned enough money to build classrooms for the Solio students.

Let's Make a Difference

Citizens decide how to take action in their communities by speaking up and listening to other people's ideas. It is important to respect what everyone has to say. Even if you do not agree with an idea, you may still learn something from it.

You have seen that kids can make a difference in their communities and in the world. Making a difference is part of being a good citizen. Whether helping to water your family's garden or raising money to buy books for a school in another country, there are many ways that you can help others.

How will you make a difference?

Learning more

Books

Hanson, Anders. *No Bullies Alowed! The Kids' Book of Dealing with Bullies.* Super Sandcastle, 2014.

Kopp, Megan. *Be the Change for the Environment.* Crabtree Publishing, 2015.

Web Sites

Find out how you can make a difference here:
www.kidscanmakeadifference.org/

Learn about a community project where kindness rules:
http://ripplekindness.org/community-project/for-kids/how-you-can-make-a-difference/

You can make a difference for children with disabilities:
www.marchofdimes.ca/EN/programs/kcmd/Pages/KCMD.aspx

Find out how you can help children around the world:
www.kidsgoglobal.net/

Words to Know

citizens (SIT-i-senz) noun People who belong to a community

community (CU-mu-ni-tee) noun A place where people live, work, and play

compromise (KOM-pruh-mahyz) noun An agreement where both sides give up something

fundraiser (FUHND-rey-zer) noun A gathering held to raise money for a cause

protest (PROH-test) noun The act of showing you do not agree with something

refugee (ref-yoo-JEE) noun A person who must leave their home country because of war or severe weather

respect (ri-SPEKT) noun To show you value the rights of others by following rules

volunteer (vol-uhn-TEER) verb To offer to help and not expect to be paid

vote (VOHT) verb Make a choice by marking a ballot or some other method such as raising your hand

A noun is a person, place, or thing.

A verb is an action word that tells you what someone or something does.

Index

About the author

Jessica Pegis is a writer and editor living in Toronto. She has written several books for teens and children in the areas of science, citizenship, and media awareness.